AI Writing Revolution

How to Use AI to Write Better, Faster, and More Creatively

ROMAN F. PRECIADO

whether such errors or omissions result from negligence, accident, or any other cause.

Table of contents

- How to use AI to generate new ideas and content
- How to use AI to improve your writing style and clarity
- How to use AI to personalize your writing for your audience

Chapter 3: Writing Faster with AI, How to use AI to automate repetitive writing tasks

- How to use AI to generate bulk content quickly
- How to use AI to edit and proofread your work efficiently
- How to use AI to help you meet deadlines

Chapter 4: Writing More Creatively with AI, How to use AI to brainstorm new ideas

- How to use AI to generate different creative text formats
- How to use AI to experiment with your writing style

- How to use AI to collaborate with other writers

Chapter 5: The Future of AI Writing, The potential of AI to revolutionize the writing process

- Ethical considerations for using AI to write
- How to prepare for the future of AI writing

Conclusion: Key takeaways from the book

- Resources for learning more about AI writing

Introduction: What is AI writing?

AI writing, also known as artificial intelligence writing, is the use of artificial intelligence (AI) to generate text. AI writing tools can be used to create a variety of content, including articles, blog posts, product descriptions, and even creative content such as poems and stories.

AI writing tools work by analyzing large amounts of data, such as text and code, to learn patterns and statistical relationships. This information is then used to generate text that is both grammatically correct and semantically meaningful.

How is AI changing the writing landscape?

AI is revolutionizing the writing landscape in several ways. First, AI writing tools can help writers to be more productive. By automating repetitive tasks, such as research and editing, AI can free up writers to focus on more creative aspects of the writing process.

Second, AI can help writers to improve their writing skills. AI writing tools can provide feedback on grammar, style, and tone. They can also help writers to identify and correct common errors.

Third, AI is making it possible for more people to write. AI writing tools can be used by anyone, regardless of their writing skills or experience. This is opening up new opportunities for businesses and individuals to create and share their content.

The benefits of using AI to write

There are several benefits to using AI to write, including:

Increased productivity: AI can help writers to be more productive by automating repetitive tasks and providing feedback on grammar, style, and tone.

Improved writing skills: AI can help writers improve their writing skills by identifying and correcting common errors.

Increased accessibility: AI makes it possible for more people to write, regardless of their writing skills or experience.

Enhanced creativity: AI can help writers to be more creative by providing new ideas and inspiration.

Who is this book for?

This book is for anyone who wants to learn how to use AI to write better, faster, and more creatively. It is especially relevant for writers, bloggers, marketers, and businesses.

This book will teach you how to choose the right AI writing software for your needs, how to use AI to improve your grammar and spelling, how to generate new ideas and content, and how to use AI to write more creatively.

You will also learn about the future of AI writing and how to prepare for the changes that are coming.

Whether you are a beginner or a seasoned writer, this book will help you take your writing skills to the next level using AI.

Chapter 1: Understanding AI Writing

In today's digital age, artificial intelligence (AI) has revolutionized various aspects of our lives, and one of the most notable domains where it's making a significant impact is writing. This chapter delves into the fundamentals of AI writing, explaining what AI is, how it functions in the context of writing, the various types of AI writing software available, and how to select the right one for your specific needs.

What is AI?

AI, or Artificial Intelligence, is a field of computer science that aims to create systems and machines that can do things that normally need human intelligence. This includes activities such as problem-solving, learning, reasoning, and decision-making. AI technology aims to replicate human cognitive functions through algorithms, data analysis, and machine learning techniques.

In the realm of writing, AI systems are designed to mimic the human capacity for language generation, allowing them to compose text, create content, and assist with a wide range of writing-related tasks.

How does AI work in the context of writing?

AI writing systems rely on complex algorithms and machine learning models to generate written content. These systems are often trained on vast datasets containing text from various sources, which enables them to understand language, context, and grammar. The key components of AI writing include:

Natural Language Processing (NLP): NLP is a crucial aspect of AI writing that focuses on the interaction between computers and human language. It enables AI to comprehend, interpret, and generate human-like text.

Machine Learning: AI writing software uses machine learning techniques to improve over time. It can analyze and adapt to user preferences, producing more accurate and contextually relevant content with each use.

Data Training: AI writing models require extensive training on a diverse set of text data to develop language proficiency. This training process refines their ability to generate coherent and contextually relevant content.

User Input: Many AI writing systems allow users to input specific instructions or prompts to guide content generation. This personalized input helps tailor the output to the user's needs.

Different types of AI writing software

AI writing software comes in various forms, each designed for different purposes. Here are some common types:

Content Generators: These tools create blog posts, articles, product descriptions, and other forms of written content.

Chatbots and Virtual Assistants: Chatbots and virtual assistants use AI to interact with users through text or speech, providing information, answering questions, and even engaging in conversations.

Grammar and Style Checkers: These tools help users improve their writing by checking for grammar, punctuation, and style errors.

Auto-Complete and Suggestion Tools: Often integrated into word processors, these tools suggest completions and corrections as users type.

Language Translation Tools: AI-driven translation software can instantly translate text between different languages with high accuracy.

How to choose the right AI writing software for you

Selecting the right AI writing software is essential to meet your specific needs and goals. To make an informed choice, consider the following factors:

Purpose: Determine what you plan to use AI writing software for, whether it's content creation, proofreading, translation, or other writing-related tasks.

Features: Evaluate the features and capabilities of different software. Look for advanced NLP, customization options, and integration with other tools or platforms.

User-Friendliness: Choose software that aligns with your proficiency level. Some AI writing tools are more user-friendly and require minimal technical expertise.

Pricing: Consider your budget and whether the software offers a free trial or subscription plans that fit your financial constraints.

Reviews and Recommendations: Read user reviews and seek recommendations from others who have used AI writing software to gain insights into its effectiveness.

Updates and Support: Ensure the software provider offers regular updates and reliable customer support.

By understanding what AI is, how it operates in the context of writing, the various types of AI writing software available, and how to choose the right one, you're better equipped to harness the power of AI to enhance your writing endeavors. This chapter sets the foundation for the journey into the world of AI writing, where the possibilities are as vast as the digital landscape itself.

Chapter 2: Writing Better with AI

AI writing tools can help you to improve your grammar and spelling in several ways. First, they can automatically detect and correct grammatical errors and spelling mistakes. Second, they can provide feedback on your writing style and clarity. Third, they can help you to learn from your mistakes so that you can avoid making them in the future.

To use AI to improve your grammar and spelling, simply run your text through an AI writing tool. The tool will identify any errors and provide suggestions for corrections. You can then review the suggestions and make the changes that you think are necessary.

Here are some specific tips for using AI to improve your grammar and spelling:

- Use the grammar and spell check features of your AI writing tool to catch any obvious errors.
- Pay attention to the feedback that your AI writing tool provides on your writing style and clarity.
- Use the suggestions from your AI writing tool to learn from your mistakes and improve your writing skills.

How to use AI to generate new ideas and content

AI writing tools can also be used to generate new ideas and content. This can be especially helpful for writers who are struggling to come up with a topic or who are having difficulty getting started on a piece of writing.

To use AI to generate new ideas and content, simply enter a few keywords or phrases into an AI writing tool. The tool will then generate a list of ideas and suggestions. You can then review the list and choose an idea that you want to develop further.

Here are some specific tips for using AI to generate new ideas and content:

- Use AI writing tools to brainstorm new topics and ideas.
- Use AI writing tools to generate outlines and drafts of your writing.
- Use AI writing tools to research information and gather evidence.

How to use AI to improve your writing style and clarity

AI writing tools can also help you to improve your writing style and clarity. This can be done by providing feedback on your sentence structure, word choice, and overall tone.

To use AI to improve your writing style and clarity, simply run your text through an AI writing tool. The tool will identify any areas where your writing can be improved and provide suggestions for changes. You can then review the suggestions and make the changes that you think are necessary.

Here are some specific tips for using AI to improve your writing style and clarity:

- Use AI writing tools to identify and correct any stylistic errors.
- Use AI writing tools to improve the readability and flow of your writing.
- Use AI writing tools to make your writing more engaging and persuasive.

How to use AI to personalize your writing for your audience

AI writing tools can also help you to personalize your writing for your audience. This can be done by analyzing your audience's interests, needs, and concerns. AI writing tools can then provide suggestions for how to tailor your writing to your audience.

To use AI to personalize your writing for your audience, simply enter a few keywords or phrases about your audience into an AI writing tool. The tool will then generate a profile of your audience and provide suggestions for how to personalize your writing for them.

Here are some specific tips for using AI to personalize your writing for your audience:

- Use AI writing tools to understand your audience's interests, needs, and concerns.
- Use AI writing tools to tailor your writing to your audience's reading level.
- Use AI writing tools to make your writing more relevant and engaging to your audience.

AI writing tools can be a valuable tool for writers of all levels of experience. By using

AI writing tools, writers can improve their grammar and spelling, generate new ideas and content, improve their writing style and clarity, and personalize their writing for their audience.

Chapter 3: Writing Faster with AI, How to use AI to automate repetitive writing tasks

AI writing tools can be used to automate a variety of repetitive writing tasks, such as:

- Writing product descriptions
- Generating social media posts
- Creating email newsletters
- Writing reports
- Creating presentations

To automate repetitive writing tasks with AI, simply identify the tasks that you want to automate and then find an AI writing tool that can help you to do them. For example, if you want to automate the process of writing product descriptions, you could use an AI writing tool that is specifically designed for this purpose.

Once you have found an AI writing tool that can help you automate your repetitive writing tasks, simply provide the tool with the necessary information and it will generate the content for you. For example, if you are using an AI writing tool to generate product descriptions, you would simply provide the tool with the product name, features, and benefits. The tool would then generate a product description for you.

How to use AI to generate bulk content quickly

AI writing tools can also be used to generate bulk content quickly. This can be especially helpful for businesses and organizations that need to create a large amount of content in a short period.

To generate bulk content quickly with AI, simply provide the AI writing tool with a topic or theme and the tool will generate a list of ideas and suggestions. You can then choose the ideas that you want to develop further and the AI writing tool will generate the content for you.

For example, if you are using an AI writing tool to generate bulk content for a blog, you could simply provide the tool with a topic or theme, such as "marketing tips." The tool would then generate a list of ideas for blog posts, such as "5 tips for writing effective marketing copy" or "How to use social media to promote your business." You could then choose the ideas that you want to develop further and the AI writing tool would generate the blog posts for you.

How to use AI to edit and proofread your work efficiently

AI writing tools can also be used to edit and proofread your work efficiently. This can be helpful for writers of all levels of experience, as it can help to catch errors and improve the overall quality of your writing.

To use AI to edit and proofread your work efficiently, simply run your text through an AI writing tool. The tool will identify any errors in grammar, spelling, punctuation, and style. It will also provide suggestions for how to improve the readability and flow of your writing.

You can then review the suggestions from the AI writing tool and make the changes that you think are necessary. This can help you to save time and produce higher-quality writing.

How to use AI to help you meet deadlines

AI writing tools can also help you to meet deadlines. By automating repetitive writing tasks and generating content quickly, AI writing tools can free up your time so that you can focus on other important tasks.

For example, if you have a deadline for a project, you can use AI to automate the process of writing product descriptions or generating social media posts. This will free up your time so that you can focus on other tasks, such as developing the product or creating a marketing plan.

Overall, AI writing tools can be a valuable tool for writers who want to write better, faster, and more creatively. By using AI writing tools, writers can automate repetitive writing tasks, generate bulk content quickly, edit and proofread their work efficiently, and meet deadlines more easily.

Chapter 4: Writing More Creatively with AI, How to use AI to brainstorm new ideas

---

AI can be used to brainstorm new ideas in a variety of ways. For example, you can use AI to:

- Generate lists of random ideas
- Combine different ideas to create new ones
- Explore different perspectives on a topic
- Develop new characters and storylines

To use AI to brainstorm new ideas, simply provide the AI with a topic or theme and the

AI will generate a list of ideas for you. You can then review the list and choose the ideas that you want to develop further.

Here are some specific tips for using AI to brainstorm new ideas:

- Use AI to generate lists of random words or phrases. You can then combine these words and phrases to create new ideas.
- Use AI to explore different perspectives on a topic. For example, if you are writing a story, you could use AI to generate ideas for different characters, settings, and plot twists.
- Use AI to develop new characters and storylines. For example, you could use AI to generate a list of character traits

and then use those traits to create a new character.

How to use AI to generate different creative text formats

AI can also be used to generate different creative text formats, such as poems, stories, scripts, and musical pieces. This can be helpful for writers who want to experiment with different forms of writing or who want to create new content for their audience.

To use AI to generate different creative text formats, simply provide the AI with the format that you want to generate and the AI will generate the content for you. For example, if you want to generate a poem, you would simply provide the AI with the topic of the poem and the AI would generate a poem for you.

Here are some specific tips for using AI to generate different creative text formats:

- Use AI to generate different types of poems, such as sonnets, limericks, and haiku.
- Use AI to generate short stories, novellas, and novels.
- Use AI to generate scripts for movies, TV shows, and plays.
- Use AI to generate musical pieces, such as songs and melodies.

How to use AI to experiment with your writing style

AI can also be used to experiment with different writing styles. This can be helpful for writers who want to find their unique voice or who want to try out different styles for different projects.

To use AI to experiment with different writing styles, simply provide the AI with a sample of your writing in a different style and the AI will generate content for you in that style. For example, if you want to experiment with writing in a more formal style, you would simply provide the AI with a sample of your writing in that style and the AI would generate content for you in that style.

Here are some specific tips for using AI to experiment with different writing styles:

- Use AI to generate content in different genres, such as fiction, non-fiction, and poetry.
- Use AI to generate content in different tones, such as formal, informal, and humorous.
- Use AI to generate content in different voices, such as first person, second person, and third person.

How to use AI to collaborate with other writers

AI can also be used to collaborate with other writers. This can be helpful for writers who want to get feedback on their work or who want to work on a project together.

To use AI to collaborate with other writers, simply share your work with the AI and the AI will provide feedback or suggestions. You can then discuss the feedback with the other writer and make changes to your work as needed.

Here are some specific tips for using AI to collaborate with other writers:

- Use AI to get feedback on your work from a different perspective.
- Use AI to brainstorm ideas with other writers.
- Use AI to co-write content with other writers.

AI can be a valuable tool for writers who want to write more creatively. By using AI to brainstorm new ideas, generate different creative text formats, experiment with their writing style, and collaborate with other writers, AI can help writers produce more creative and innovative work.

Chapter 5: The Future of AI Writing, The potential of AI to revolutionize the writing process

AI has the potential to revolutionize the writing process in several ways. First, AI can help writers to be more productive by automating repetitive tasks and providing feedback on grammar, style, and clarity. Second, AI can help writers to improve their writing skills by identifying and correcting common errors. Third, AI can help writers to be more creative by providing new ideas and inspiration.

Here are some specific examples of how AI is already being used to revolutionize the writing process:

- AI-powered writing assistants can help writers with a variety of tasks, such as generating outlines, writing product descriptions, and creating social media posts.
- AI-powered grammar and spelling checkers can help writers to identify and correct errors in their writing.
- AI-powered style guides can help writers to improve the readability and clarity of their writing.
- AI-powered creativity tools can help writers to generate new ideas and inspiration.

As AI continues to develop, it is likely to become even more powerful and versatile. This means that AI has the potential to revolutionize the writing process in ways that we cannot even imagine today.

Ethical considerations for using AI to write

Several ethical considerations need to be taken into account when using AI to write. One concern is that AI could be used to create fake news or propaganda. Another concern is that AI could be used to write content that is discriminatory or offensive.

Using AI ethically and responsibly is very important. Here are some tips:

- Be transparent about the use of AI. When you use AI to write content, be sure to disclose this to your audience.

- Use AI to supplement your writing skills, not to replace them. AI is a powerful tool, but it is not a substitute for human creativity and judgment.

- Be mindful of the potential for bias in AI. AI writing tools are trained on large amounts of data, and this data can contain bias. We need to be mindful of this possible bias and take actions to reduce it.

- Use AI to write content that is ethical and responsible. Avoid using AI to write content that is fake news, propaganda, discriminatory, or offensive.

How to prepare for the future of AI writing

As AI continues to develop, it is important to be prepared for the changes that are coming. Here are some tips:

- Stay up-to-date on the latest advances in AI writing, like Chatgpt 4.0. This will help you to understand how AI is being used to write content and how it is likely to impact you in the future.
- Learn how to use AI writing tools effectively. This will help you to take advantage of the benefits of AI writing while avoiding the potential pitfalls.
- Develop your writing skills. Even as AI becomes more powerful, human creativity and judgment will still be

essential for writing high-quality content.

By following these tips, you can prepare for the future of AI writing and ensure that you are well-positioned to succeed.

AI is rapidly changing the world around us, and the writing process is no exception. AI has the potential to revolutionize the way we write, making it easier, faster, and more creative. However, it is important to use AI responsibly and ethically. By staying up-to-date on the latest advances in AI writing, learning how to use AI writing tools effectively, and developing your writing skills, you can prepare for the future of AI writing and ensure that you are well-positioned to succeed.

Conclusion: Key takeaways from the book

AI writing is a powerful tool that can help writers to be more productive, improve their writing skills, and be more creative.

AI writing tools can be used to automate repetitive tasks, provide feedback on grammar, style, and clarity, generate new ideas and inspiration, and create different creative text formats.

It is important to use AI writing responsibly and ethically. This means being transparent about the use of AI, using AI to supplement your writing skills, being mindful of the potential for bias in AI, and using AI to write content that is ethical and responsible.

To prepare for the future of AI writing, it is important to stay up-to-date on the latest advances in AI writing, learn how to use AI writing tools effectively, and develop your writing skills.

Resources for learning more about AI writing

Here are some resources for learning more about AI writing:

Books:

AI Writing Revolution: How to Use AI to Write Better, Faster, and More Creatively by Bard

The AI-Powered Writer: How to Write Better, Faster, and Smarter with Artificial Intelligence by Robbie Allen

AI Writing Assistants: How to Use AI to Improve Your Writing by Chris Brogan

Websites:

AI Writing Resources: A comprehensive list of AI writing tools and resources

The Future of AI Writing: A blog about the latest trends and developments in AI writing

AI Writing Case Studies: A collection of case studies on how AI is being used to write content in different industries

Courses:

AI for Writers: A course on how to use AI to improve your writing skills

The AI Writing Masterclass: A course on how to use AI to write better content, faster

The AI Writer's Bootcamp: A course on how to get started with AI writing